VOLUME · GEOMETRY · COLOR

House Design

REGINA PIZZININI &
LEON LUXEMBURG

VOLUME·GEOMETRY·COLOR

House Design

REGINA PIZZININI &
LEON LUXEMBURG

2

TEXT BY MICHAEL WEBB   FOREWORD BY BUZZ YUDELL

First published in Australia in 1998 by
The Images Publishing Group Pty Ltd
ACN 059 734 431
6 Bastow Place, Mulgrave, Victoria 3170, Australia
Telephone +(61 3) 9561 5544 Facsimile +(61 3) 9561 4860
E-mail: books@images.com.au

National Library of Australia Cataloguing-in-Publication Data

Webb, Michael, 1937–.
Pizzinini/Luxemburg.

Bibliography.
Includes index.
ISBN 1 86470 002 5.

House Design Series ISSN 1329 0045

1. Pizzinini, Regina, 1959–. 2. Luxemburg, Leon, 1955–.
3. Architecture, Domestic – Designs and plans.
I. Pizzinini, Regina, 1959–. II. Luxemburg, Leon, 1955–.
III. Title. (Series : House Design: 2).

728.0222

Edited by Kerry Cannon

Designed by The Graphic Image Studio Pty Ltd
Mulgrave, Australia

Printed in Hong Kong

FOREWORD

by Buzz Yudell

Leon brightly attired, Regina poised all in black or perhaps in searing reds, this creative couple appears and vanishes from two continents as effortlessly as the Lone Ranger and Tonto. In their wake are sprouting an enticing set of colorful jewels which embody the same energy, delight, surprise and complexities of this dynamic design duo.

Nearly 15 years ago they appeared in Los Angeles to immerse themselves in the closest thing to the anti-world of their traditional European background, and specifically to study with the puckish guru they correctly expected Charles Moore to be. Their first interview with Charles was prophetic.

He, laid up with back pain, nonetheless insisted that they visit him at his recently completed condominium. Regina and Leon climbed up the great meandering stair which is the soul of the house, to be received by Charles, nearly immobile on his back. The pair came presciently prepared with both a portfolio of student work and an exotically rich multi-layered torte. For the duration of the meeting Leon and Regina took turns holding boards of their work horizontally upside down for the supine Charles Moore to see while he encouraged the other to feed him pieces of pastry. To this day they are uncertain if Charles's moans of appreciation were for the cake, their portfolio or both.

He was sufficiently impressed to instruct them to appear at our office and "suggest to Buzz and John that they work for us". Thus my partner John Ruble and I were first introduced to the pair, this time, alas, torteless.

We were by now accustomed to young architects appearing in our office with vague representations that Charles had sent them. Lacking a plan for how best to employ them we asked if they could model a piece of the concept design for our Humboldt Library set on the Tegel Harbor in Berlin. As a European project it was dimensioned metrically, which we thought would allow for an easier fit with their training.

As Leon recalls, John and I quickly vanished into the fog of other projects and meetings and they were left with little instruction about scale, size and details required for their model. Unlike most new employees, their take on how to survive this dilemma was to plunge ahead without struggling to ascertain our detailed expectations. They worked feverishly through the night and all through the weekend so that on Monday morning we entered the office to find an enormous finished model of the entire Library, a model of far grander scale and detail than we could ever have expected. This was the beginning of a long professional and personal relationship which has always been characterized by a joie de vivre matched by an equal joie d'oeuvre.

Catching California

Leon and Regina came to California not just to observe it but to live it. Whether as graduate students at UCLA, as collaborators in our office or as consumers of the culture and landscape of the region, they immersed themselves with gusto in the experience. They took naturally to the open, informal and exploratory nature of the culture. They claim to have learned the pleasures of creative and non-hierarchical collaboration from working in our office. They began to live the expansive life of California not as

an alternative to their European experience, but as a complement to it. Like Charles Moore they constantly reveled in the diversity of place and culture. They began to explore Mexico and Central America with the open eyes and mind of youth. Multilingual and endlessly adventurous, they were equally at home in any part of the world.

When the time came to begin their own practice it seemed natural to them to have offices in both Europe and California. The already daunting and laborious process of building a practice was further weighted with the logistics of maintaining studios in Santa Monica, Luxembourg and eventually Vienna, not to mention residences near each office. But with their impish charm masking wills of steel they persevered through logistic, financial and professional challenges to build a unique kind of practice and a fresh and exuberant body of work.

Getting the Yin and Yang of it

Charles Moore always spoke of the pleasure of dualities in architecture. He loved mixing materials that were plain and fancy, scales that were grand and diminutive, elements that were aggressively yang or soothingly yin. Leon and Regina were soulmates in their appreciation of this inclusiveness. With roots in their European schooling and the careful Cartesian making of buildings, and their reach into the experiential and sensuous approach to habitation of Charles and the West, they have been able to create a joyous yet anchored synthesis. Their work celebrates habitation with spatial surprises, stairways that link the earth and sky, bays that beckon us to sit and to view. At the same time it is built with an old world love of craft, an appreciation for tectonics and a stablizing reliance on Platonic forms.

Regina, whose ancestors include a line of craftsmen expert in gold-leafing church interiors, has continued this connection to craft. She cut a striking figure several years ago when, working with Tina Beebe on a ceiling collage in our Church of the Nativity, she asked to be hoisted some 40 feet into the air in the bucket of a cherry picker, there to stay hours on end while she painstakingly applied gold leaf to the ceiling. She was characteristically undaunted by the overt amusement of the hard-hatted workers. Both Leon and Regina can be found on a weekend building a stairway to their roof garden, designing and building furniture, testing colors in a client's house and later kayaking in the Pacific, watching dolphins or barbecuing on the beach. I suspect that in Europe they are equally successful as cross-pollinators.

New World Orders Taken Here

It is a pleasure to see such an energetic and creative couple innovate and improvise their way to new models for making architecture in the flux of our geographically contracting and technologically expanding world. They look to their past with appreciation and to the future with exhilaration. Their aplomb in juggling present complexities and welcoming future uncertainties is inspiring. Their compass is constantly set to making places which connect us to our surroundings, delight, surprise and nurture us.

Photo: Regina and Leon with Charles Moore at one of his birthday parties (which he celebrated on Halloween)

CONTENTS

INTRODUCTION

Josef Lackner, school

Opening off the tarmac of Santa Monica Airport is a hangar that outshines any flying machine; a painted cave that is half concealed by executive jets and the vintage planes of an aviation museum. Blue stairs, flanked by a red bay and a yellow wall, slice up to an open gallery, and architectural models are clustered on every free surface. This is the studio of Regina Pizzinini and Leon Luxemburg, who spend half their time designing here, and then return to their home bases in Europe to build, leaving Iceland-born Tryggvi Thorsteinsson to run the office.

These part-time émigrés are putting a fresh spin on an old story, for Los Angeles has always been full of inventive people who have flocked here from around the world to realize their dreams. Eighty years ago, hopefuls clustered at the gates of the movie studios, eager to be noticed or to slip past the guards. Richard Neutra and Rudolph Schindler journeyed from Vienna to work with Frank Lloyd Wright and then made their mark by adapting European modernism to southern California. Arnold Schoenberg and Igor Stravinsky, Thomas Mann and Berthold Brecht were among the refugees, celebrated and obscure, who fled here from Nazi-occupied Europe. More recently, the workshops and warehouses of West LA, abandoned by blue-collar trades, have been appropriated by designers in blue jeans, who generate ideas, images, and illusions. Cutting-edge architects have located their studios in the lofts of Culver City, Santa Monica, and Venice.

For all these talents, opportunity was the lure—the chance to make a fresh start in a wide-open city that is unconstrained by tradition. Regina and Leon, newly graduated from the University of Innsbruck Architecture School, arrived in 1983. They taught and studied for their Masters degrees, worked in the Moore Ruble Yudell office, and launched their practice by building a guest house for film producers Roger and Julie Corman. Since then, they have designed a film studio and a church, a restaurant and a concert hall, while constantly returning to residential jobs. They have built houses for themselves, remodeled old structures, planned public housing, and developed lasting relationships with satisfied clients. Geometric forms, soaring volumes, and primary colors are the themes on which they have played a witty series of variations. Both teach at UCLA and in Europe, and offer part-time jobs to their students, as Moore did for them.

Chance brought them together in Austria and shaped their international careers. Regina was born in the Tirolese mountain village of Niederthai. Her father was a painter, but she planned to become a doctor, and studied Latin as one of the first two girls in the nearby monastery school at Stams. Impulsively, she switched to architecture when she went to university. Leon joined the same class, after spending much of his childhood in Luxembourg improvising shelters of every kind. Inspired by his architect

uncle, and by the story of four young men who spent the war in an ingenious cave dwelling to elude the Germans, the boy built an ambitious structure of pine trunks, nailed boards, and broom for his sister. He was 11 and the house survives in his mother's garden, alongside a studio apartment he built for himself 27 years later. Leon also tried to construct a submarine from a water tank during a family holiday in Spain, but he lacked the academic skills to become an engineer and went off to architecture school as a last resort, choosing Innsbruck because his sister was studying medicine there.

He and Regina soon became inseparable friends, learning to collaborate during the year they spent restoring a ruined hunting lodge that overlooks the city. It had been built for the Emperor Maximilian, and was owned by the local doctors' association, which hoped to redevelop it as a vacation complex. Ten students banded together to rent it for their five years of school, and did such an impressive job of repair that they were able to get the building listed as a historic monument and taken off the market–much to the doctors' chagrin. The skills Leon had honed building cabins were now applied to a 17-room castle, and to the buried water tank that they turned into a swimming pool.

When they returned to school from this productive sabbatical, they found new opportunities to soar. Field trips to northern Italy inspired a love of tight-knit hill towns. Josef Lackner, an innovative Innsbruck architect, completed a radical school building and became a professor, inspiring his students to experiment with structural forms. Another teacher based his course on the writings of Charles Moore, exploring the way that paths, staircases, roofs, windows and other elements come together in a building. Moore had just completed the Piazza d'Italia in New Orleans, a joyful explosion of Italianate forms animated by neon and running water, and that spurred the pair to spend some time in the United States.

The two hopefuls applied to 40 schools: Leon secured a teaching assistant position at the University of Houston, Regina at the University of Southern California. It was a rude shock to arrive in these vast urban sprawls, knowing no-one, having little money and no wheels. Leon experienced the aftermath of a devastating hurricane that left the streets paved with shards of glass, and spent his first weekend riding public buses and trying to make sense of the city. Regina landed at Burbank airport, took a bus to a deserted downtown, and a taxi to a campus marooned in a high-crime area. Their excitement at breaking loose abruptly faded.

Within a few months, their situation had dramatically improved. Both transferred to UCLA where Moore became their professor. Regina remembers how she had to screw up her courage to call him "Charles", rather than "Mr Professor" in the European way. Their Austrian teachers had been harsh critics; here they encountered positive reinforcement in design studios. They joined Moore on study trips around southern California, where they discovered the legacy of Schindler, Neutra and the still-active John Lautner, and to the woodsy settlement of Sea Ranch on the northern Californian coast. Visits to Mexico exposed them to pyramids and the houses of Luis Barragan, strong colors, the interweaving of cultures, and the exuberant celebrations on the Day of the Dead. Later trips, to China and Yemen, inspired a love of the simple geometric shapes that provide building blocks in every indigenous architectural tradition. Meanwhile, they worked on MRY's Tegel project in Berlin–Leon on the housing, Regina on the library–for four years after getting their masters degrees.

That experience taught them they could practice anywhere, flying from LA to Europe, as Moore constantly did, in the same time it would take to drive from Vienna to Luxembourg. It also reinforced their enthusiasm for collaboration ("in the six years we were in that office the staff grew from 15 to 60 but we never heard a voice raised in anger", recalls Leon), and for the importance of joy and exuberance in architecture. They realized they could have a productive career in America and in Europe, enjoying the freedom of LA while satisfying the tug of roots and families.

Their first commission was referred to them by Yudell and by another UCLA instructor, cultural historian Charles Jencks. Photographs of the vivid, intriguingly sculpted Corman Guest House were widely published and stirred interest in their work. However, the timing was bad, for California and Europe were undergoing a severe recession, and the firm was able to realize only small projects and remodels for several years.

Leon opened an office in the City of Luxembourg. He had taken the name of his birthplace for himself in the United States as a marketing tool for a range of concrete furniture that he and Regina had designed. Back home, he reverted to the family name of Glodt, and designed a tiny studio, aptly named Villa Petite, in the garden of his mother's house. Regina took over a top-floor apartment in the heart of the old city of Vienna, creating a duplex *pied à terre* in one half and a studio in the other. They began to establish the work rhythm that has sustained them ever since: three weeks designing together in LA, alternating with three back in Europe, where they supervise current projects and seek new commissions from their respective offices. "To accomplish something you have to be liberated from familiar surroundings", says Leon. "Going away gives you fresh energy." Weekends are spent together in Austria or Luxembourg.

The pattern has intensified now that each has collaborated on the design of an ambitious house for the other on his or her home ground. Regina works in Vienna, but her heart (and family) remain in Niederthai, and it is there that she has created a soaring cubist cabin of wood and stucco-clad concrete block with a bowed metal roof. Leon's house, located four miles from his birthplace, is outwardly more conservative. It began as a project for his sister and her daughter, but they moved away, and now he has taken the spacious, multilevel loft for himself. The partners have also converted a couple of town houses and an old barn and built a studio for a commercial photographer in different parts of Luxembourg. These ventures inspired an ambitious house in the German capital of Bonn, and that led to another commission in the same neighborhood. They are waiting to begin a major public housing project for the city of Vienna and, back in LA, they have recently extended a bungalow for the German-born chef, Hans Röckenwagner.

After 20 years of friendship and collaboration, each finds it hard to define what the other does. Every job presents a fresh challenge and leads on to the next, like a plant pushing up a stem and putting out leaves. The working method seldom changes. It may begin with a sketch, which is turned into a study model. Over a period of three weeks, they bat ideas back and forth until they have reached agreement. Leon believes you have to look for one special thing in each job: a single good idea can make a house; too many can spoil it. They have a rule that neither can change a final model without the other's agreement. Generally, this model serves as the basis for working drawings and each takes turns as project architect, seeing projects through to completion.

Common to all their jobs is a sense of volume and verticality. Moore would put tiny rooms within rooms to create the illusion of space in the tightest of frames, and string them along a staircase that became a stepped linear room, lined with bookshelves and places to gather.

Meinhardinum Stift Stams, school-monastery restored by Franz Xaver Pizzinini with Anton Pizzinini

Sea Ranch

Grödner Joch, Italian Alps

Regina and Leon layer space with cut-away screen walls, suspend volumes within lofty interiors, and employ precipitous, unrailed stairs to add to the sense of height and provide the thrill of vertigo. Regina's early experience of mountains is evident in everything they do.

Another theme is color, which is used as boldly as in the buildings of the pioneer German modernist Bruno Taut, the De Stijl designers Gerrit Rietveld and Theo Van Doesberg, and, of course, Luis Barragán and his direct heir, Ricardo Legorreta. Those are the obvious affinities, but there is no sense of mimicry in their work. Regina was inspired by painted village churches, the blaze of red geraniums that enlivens the wooden balconies of Tirolese houses, and the reductive geometry of Kasimir Malevitch and Piet Mondrian. For Leon, coming from the gray north, color offers an alternative to elaborate detail; it provides an inexpensive means of articulating forms and setting one plane off from another. When he first visited Regina's house in Niederthai, he looked first for the red stairs, fearing she might have had second thoughts, and shouted "She did it! She said she would do it and she did!" However, there is a price to be paid for these sharp-edged compositions–regular repainting in the approved hues of red, yellow, and blue, with occasional touches of purple and green.

"Every client is different", says Regina. "We try to give them something they didn't imagine, pushing them a little to accept tall, open spaces, with varied views and levels, and hope they can adapt their habits, and will find the experience rewarding. To sleep in a glass-fronted cube can give you the sense of flying. What's important is to come back to something that's so special that it makes you feel alive." For Leon, "a house is like a friend, that you should revisit regularly to be sure it's well and to enjoy its company."

The text by Michael Webb was developed from his article on Regina Pizzinini and Leon Luxemburg, published by *Metropolis* magazine (New York) in Spring, 1998.

Mexico

Niederthai, painting by Franz Xaver Pizzinini

CORMAN GUEST HOUSE

Santa Monica, California, USA
Design/Completion 1989/1992

1

Vibrant red retaining walls and yellow skylights emerge from an expanse of lawn at the end of the Cormans' garden, inviting you to explore the downslope, descend the yellow stairs and enter the tiny green apartment to the left or the intense blue studio to the right. After the cool white expanses of the main house, it's like walking into a field of color. The stairs are only three feet wide; when the walls reflect the sun, the color is penetrating, and you feel the increase in temperature. At the bottom it's cooler, and the interiors, with their soft colors and natural materials, feel calm and intimate after the drama of the descent. A whimsical metal canopy juts from the studio; within, a cradle of beams filters the skylight. Studio and apartment have decks overlooking a golf course, and they open up to breezes off the ocean, a mile away.

It was Julie Corman who invited Regina and Leon to sketch three different designs for a guest house that she could give her husband as a birthday present, allowing him to choose which one to build. As a prolific, low-budget film director and producer, Roger Corman had launched the careers of Jack Nicholson, Francis Coppola, and Martin Scorsese, and he gave his fledgling architects a good start, holding brisk on-site meetings, and encouraging them to go the limit. Later, he commissioned them to design a film studio in Ireland—though this proved too costly for his bare-bones company.

From the start, the architects sought to stir emotions. The sudden explosion of color recalls the moment in *The Wizard of Oz*, when Dorothy realizes she is not in Kansas any more, and the elements of surprise and procession recall the hallucinatory movies that Roger Corman himself directed. The 1,950-square foot (210-square meter) building provided a quiet retreat for his guests, and a place where he could be alone to paint or read a book. Later, the studio would serve as a rumpus room for the Cormans' teenage sons. In all these roles, this bold

Continued...

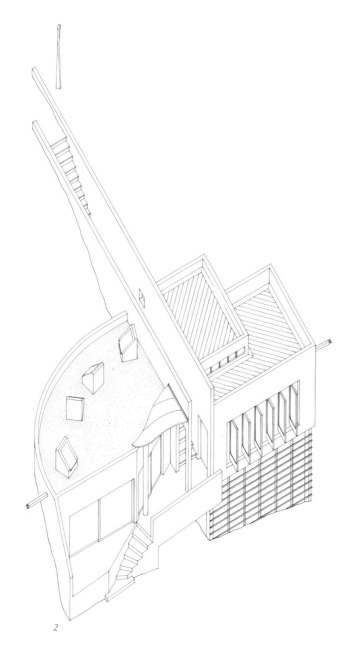

2

1   Library and red walls from the side
2   Axonometric
Opposite:
    Exterior red walls flank yellow steps

4

miniature shows how much can be achieved at minimal expense, through the manipulation of mood and scale.

The structure, here and in the architects' other buildings, is generic: wood-frame in California; insulated concrete block and poured-in-place concrete slab in Europe. The frames are clad in cement stucco and painted.

4   Looking down onto roof as viewed
    from main house
5   Exterior detail
Opposite:
    Looking into the library towards the blue balcony

5

VILLA PETITE

Bridel, Luxembourg
Design/Completion 1991/1993

1

2

This stand-alone house, half-hidden among the mature trees in Leon's mother's garden, was designed while construction was proceeding on the Corman Guest House, and a spirit of play links the two projects. There is an *Alice in Wonderland* feeling about the double sweep of yellow stairs, projecting red bay, and jauntily tilted circular roof. They dominate the 18-foot-square gray stucco block, making it seem much larger than it is, and the fanned logs that appear to support the roof relate it to the trunks that surround it. The interior is a marvel of compression that feels expansive, for the modest interiors are flooded with light from the huge windows, and borrow space from the garden. A double garage occupies the base. You climb the yellow steps to a blue door, ascend blue stairs to a stepped yellow bridge and an angled screen wall, ending up in the red sleeping bay. From there, you can enjoy every shift of the light and the seasons, observing sunlight and snow, rain and falling leaves as though you were sitting inside a telescope. The bay was designed to face north, so that the view is always backlit. All this is incorporated in just 335 square feet (36 square meters).

"The less room you occupy, the more is left to look at", remarks Leon. "We realized that this was the scale we felt comfortable handling at that time." The architects constructed a model and cut out quarter-inch-high cardboard figures to show how people would relate to the interiors, and moved the levels up and down to enhance the spatial experience and achieve a human scale. The same approach was used to balance the colors and the solid forms within the void and upon the facades. It was a learning experience with a productive outcome. Leon lived there on visits home until he moved to his new house. The Villa Petite is now rented out, and has proved entirely self-sufficient.

1   Detail through trees
2   Sketch of Villa Petite
3   House and garden

3

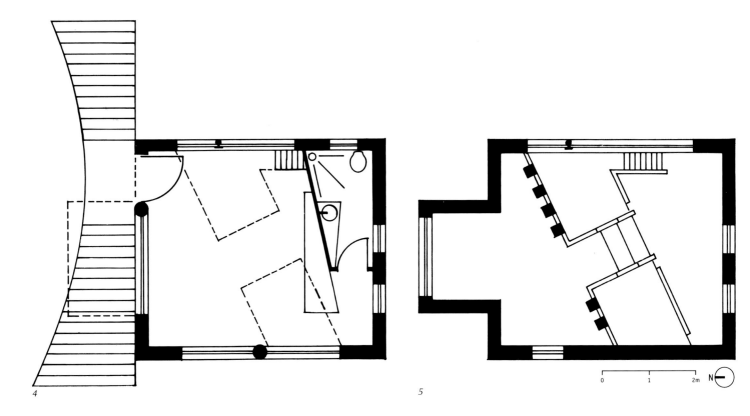

4   Studio floor plan
5   Loft floor plan
6   Interior view from blue intermediate level to inside of red cube
Opposite:
    Interior view of main floor with yellow bridge above

EICH APARTMENTS

City of Luxembourg, Luxembourg
Design/Completion 1992/1994

The owner of a single-family townhouse near the center of Luxembourg commissioned Regina and Leon to convert it to furnished rental units for single professionals working in the city on six-month visas. The three-story house was built in 1920, and its yellow stucco street facade was left unchanged. The interior was gutted, and the original masonry was framed in yellow stucco alongside a new three-foot-wide staircase that links the three units. It suggests a steep and narrow street in the old town.

Windows in each unit open onto this stair hall, creating the illusion of another room, and making the interiors (nine feet wide by 22 feet deep) feel more spacious.

The building's 335 square feet (36 square meters) have been divided to give each unit an enclosed bedroom and bathroom, and a kitchenette opening out of the living space. Fireplaces have been added, and the top unit is a duplex, with a sleeping gallery tucked into the attic story.

The lateral division is expressed in the new boldly colored garden facade: yellow for the stairs, a red window wall and a purple chimney indicating the width of the apartments. The lower unit opens onto the upper level of the garden; occupants of the top units have access to the lower garden beside a river.

1   First sketch
2   Former garden facade
Opposite:
*   New garden facade*

4

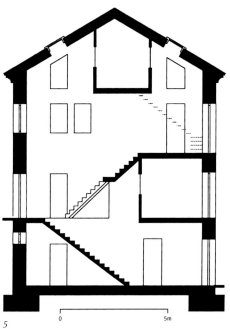

5

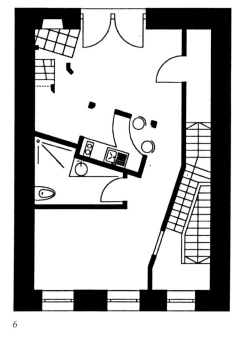

6

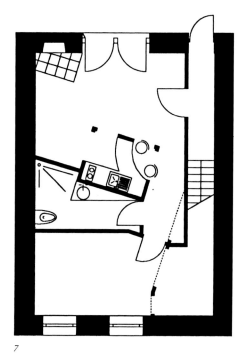

7

8

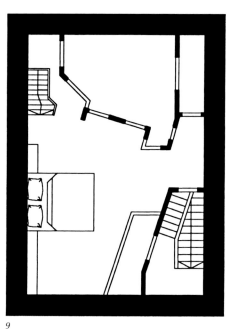

9

4   Interior common stair looking up to entrance level
     of top unit
5   Section
6   Floor plan, entrance level
7   Floor plan, garden level
8   Floor plan, upper level
9   Floor plan, loft
10   Interior common stair: windows overlooking
     the space

10

KIRCH APARTMENTS

Mamer, Luxembourg
Design/Completion 1994/1996

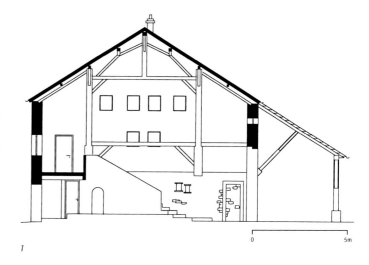

1

2

The owner of this 200-year-old barn considered tearing it down and redeveloping the site, before he saw the Eich apartments and commissioned Regina and Leon to convert the massive building. It is located in a country town, five miles from the city, and adjoins a farmhouse that was built as a dependency of a castle.

Haywains drove into the central void through a tall rounded arch, and their loads were forked into the stables on either side—one of which had earlier been adapted for use by a farmworker. The architects restored this lofty space, cleaning rough stone walls and hand-hewn oak beams, replacing the planks of the roof and installing a

skylight. To either side they created single-story apartments, one of them currently used for common storage, and a staircase that leads up to a duplex apartment to either side.

The street front and duplex facades have been plastered in the same yellow stucco as the farmhouse, and their windows open onto the great hall with its chandelier, appropriating the space in much the same way as the Eich units borrow from the staircase. From the stairs, these inner facades read as two houses facing each other across a street.

Continued...

1   Section
2   New entrance facade
3   Lobby before remodelling

3

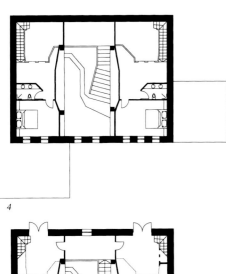

4

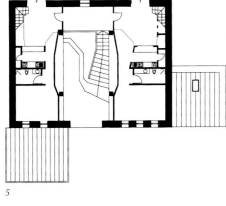

5

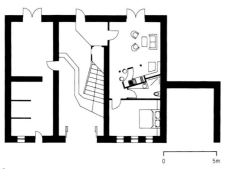

0   5m

6

The unfurnished apartments are twice the size of those at Eich, with a combined area of 1,812 square feet (195 square meters). They have been rented to couples. The duplexes have open galleries and pierced screen walls enclosing skylit spaces one can walk through. The light models the columns, articulates the space and achieves an ethereal, immaterial effect that contrasts sharply with the bold colored geometry of the Corman House and the Villa Petite. These cool interiors complement the grand scale and rough textures of the historic fabric.

4   Plan, loft level
5   Plan, upper level
6   Plan, entrance level
7&8 Interior details of layered elevation
9   New lobby

7

8

9

MERSCH HOUSE

City of Luxembourg, Luxembourg
Design/Completion 1995/1996

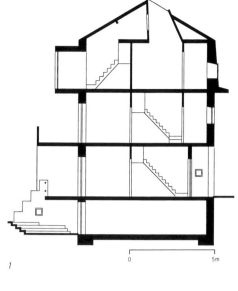

1

Ten minutes' walk from the city center is a quarter that once housed artisans and workshops, but has recently been gentrified. Houses face onto a linear park that was formerly occupied by a monastery, and rest on the foundations of a medieval fortress. A doctor and his journalist wife moved into a cramped 1930 row house and commissioned Regina and Leon to remodel it. The architects decided to restore the best of the original, with its handsome street facade, Italian terrazzo floors, and art deco metalwork. Everything to the rear was changed, increasing usable space in the 18 x 30-foot house by a third, to a total area of 2,508 square feet (270 square meters).

A blue amphitheater opens up the former basement, now the living area, to the tiny triangle of the back yard. A semicircular yellow balcony pushes out from the master bedroom on the middle level, and an 8-foot-tall red cube extends from the former attic story. These additions animate the rear wall and blur the division between indoors and out. The interior was gutted, and a two-story loft was inserted in the attic. The lower level serves as a library and office so that the wife can work at home and keep an eye on her small son as he plays in the house or the yard. A steep stair leads up to a cozy retreat occupying the space beneath a yellow skylight that illuminates the staircase.

1   Section
2   Garden facade with flowers
3   Garden facade with city in background

2

3

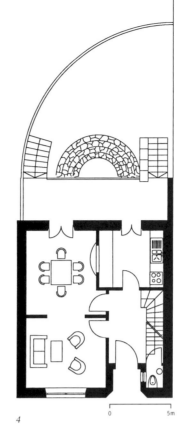

4   Plan, garden level
5   Garden facade viewed from below
Opposite:
     Garden terraces, viewed from above

4

0   5m

5

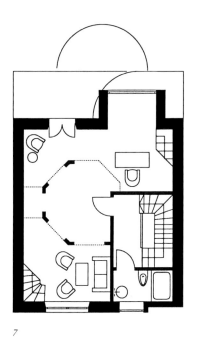

7

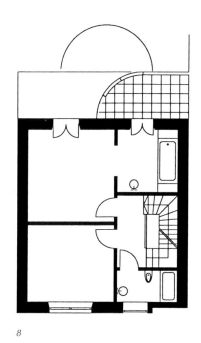

8

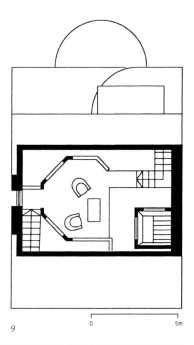

0   5m

9

10

11

7   Plan, third floor level
8   Plan, upper floor level
9   Plan, loft level
10 View into yellow skylight from main stair
11 Detail of interior of red cube
12 Detail of yellow skylight on loft level
Opposite:
    Interior of lower loft level

12

KIEFFER
PHOTO STUDIO

City of Luxembourg, Luxembourg
Design/Completion 1994/1996

1

This was the first building to take the architects' colored geometry from gardens and interiors to a public street located in a suburban district of Luxembourg. It looks like a house, but is actually a studio for photographer Jean-Paul Kieffer, who does everything but sleep there. Even so, the design might have run into trouble except for the fact that, in Europe, plans are submitted and approved in black and white. As at Villa Petite, colored volumes project from a 40 x 40-foot gray stucco box that is flared along one side to follow the building line. A tapered yellow tower marks the entrance, a red frame marks the upstairs office that is the domain of Jean-Paul's wife, Claire, with a purple skylight above her desk. The red frame reappears to the rear, where the glass is mirrored to create an optical illusion. Every angle of the 1,143-square foot (123-square meter) building, and the exuberant sculpture in the forecourt, draws attention and offers a gift to the street.

The studio itself occupies most of the interior: a 20-foot-high white box with north light and rounded corners to achieve an effect of infinity. Cars can be driven in for photo sessions through a roll-up door, and Jean-Paul can gain distance by shooting diagonally across the space or from the gallery. Clients can wait at the brushed-steel bar above the entrance, and stairs lead up to the flat roof, which can be used for outdoor shoots. The office skylight is filtered by a cradle of beams—a device first used in the Corman library. Color is used as a discreet accent to preserve the clarity of light in the studio. A basement contains a changing/make-up area for models, storage, and a professional darkroom.

2

1 Exterior detail with mirror, side elevation
2 View of exterior
Opposite:
    Gallery with bar and blue stairs

4

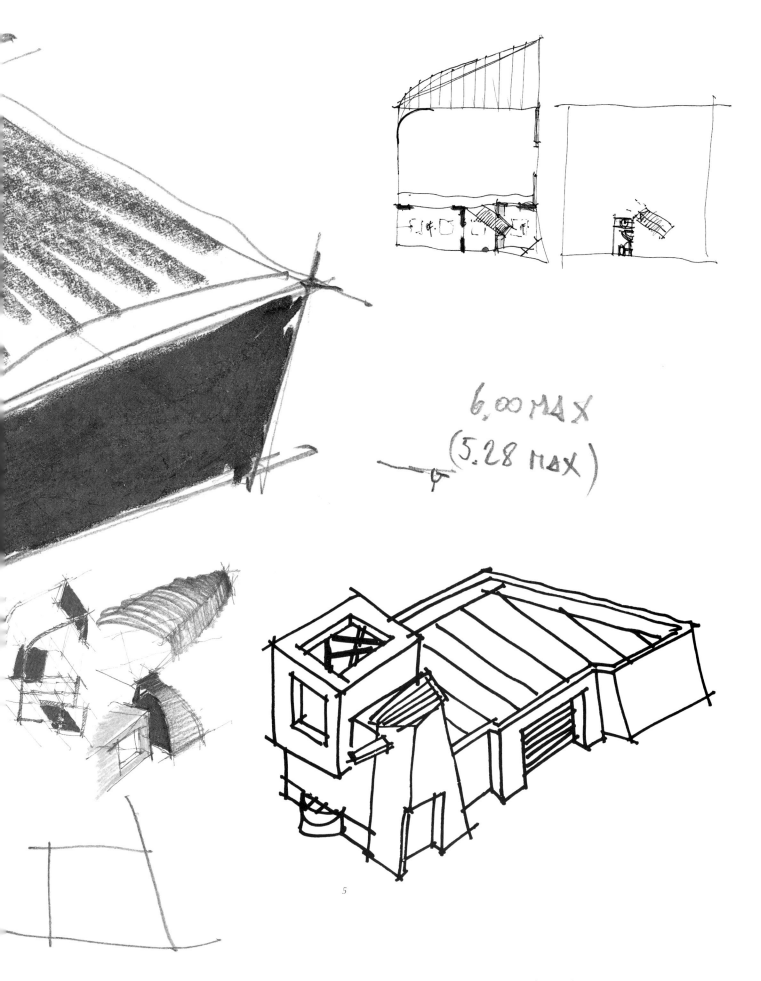

6,00 MAX

(5.28 MAX)

5

4   Preliminary sketches
5   Axonometric

6　Section
7　Interior of studio
8　Gallery with office, skylight and wooden
　shading beams

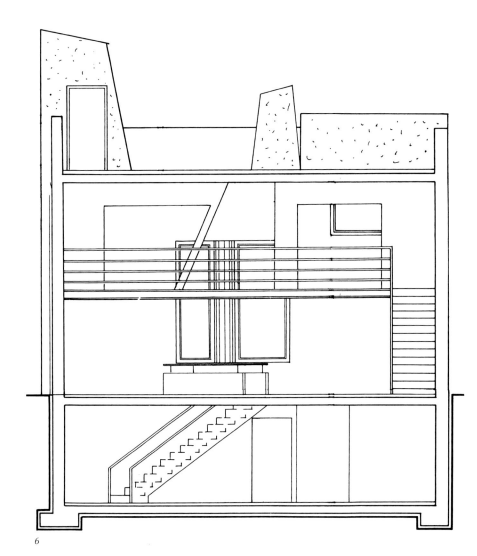

6

7

8

HOUSE, SCHOENFELS

Schoenfels, Luxembourg
Design/Completion 1993/1997

1

2

1 House on hillside
2 View from living room towards yellow arch
Opposite:
    View from mezzanine towards top floor with Iceland
    pony rug on the floor

Leon's new house has the same 40-foot-square footprint as the Kieffer studio, and is located only a mile away, but is radically different in every other respect. It was commissioned by his sister, an anesthesiologist, who planned to live there with her 11-year-old daughter, and invited Leon to "do something wonderful". Despite the difference of age, the two women treated each other like girlfriends, and that suggested a loft-like volume in which each would have her own space and be able to choose privacy or participation by emerging into shared areas. As he and Regina worked on the design, Leon imagined living there with his own son or niece, and when his sister's job took her to another city, he inherited the project and felt entirely comfortable. "We always build for ourselves and find that other people enjoy the same experiences. Here, I'm usually alone, and I can live in one room while seeing and feeling the entire house", he says. "There's nothing I want to change."

The house occupies a prominent hillside site, looking east to a village and an old castle, and this traditional setting dictated the regular windows in a pink stucco facade and the pitched slate roof. Stepping inside is a shock, for nothing prepares you for the fluid, labyrinthine quality of the interior. Color is sparingly used, to emphasize the cubic volume of the house and the interplay of angles and curves. The design of the 5,202-square foot (560-square meter) house began with a grid of nine squares, which were stretched and rotated. An open-sided cube containing the living room is skewed within the larger volume, stairs run up at an angle beneath a rounded arch, folded screens (carried over from the scored cardboard in the study model) define galleries. Casement windows in these screen walls mimic those on the perimeter, and it is easy to open one and look down through the house from either of the upper levels. The house offers a kinesthetic experience, a three-dimensional puzzle, a dance of the veils.

Continued...

4   *Plan, ground level*
5   *Plan, top level*
6   *Dining room*

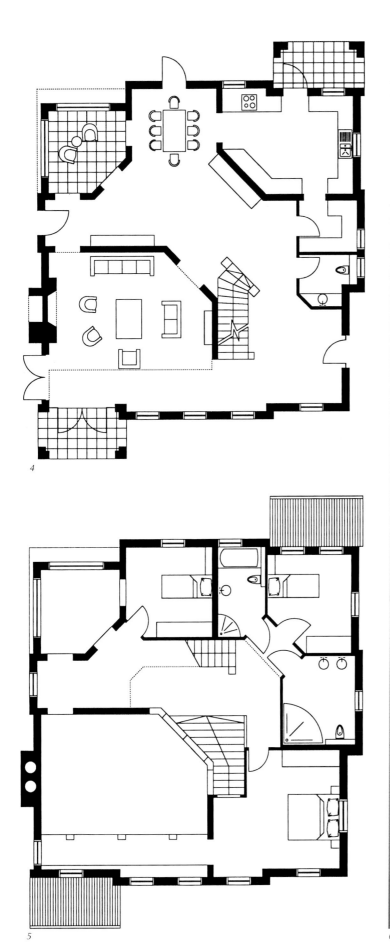

4

5

6

For the first time in their short career, the architects could indulge in the luxury of space and a freedom to shape it as they pleased—though the house contains all the amenities one would expect. Early-morning sun penetrates every space through the east-facing windows, and floods in through skylights during the rest of the day. The house feels luminous and subtly layered even on dull days, which, in Luxembourg, are all too frequent.

7

8

9

7   Open sided stairs linking the three levels
8   View towards fireplace with striped sofa
9   Looking down into living room

PIZZININI
STUDIO/APARTMENT

Vienna, Austria
Design/Completion 1995/1997

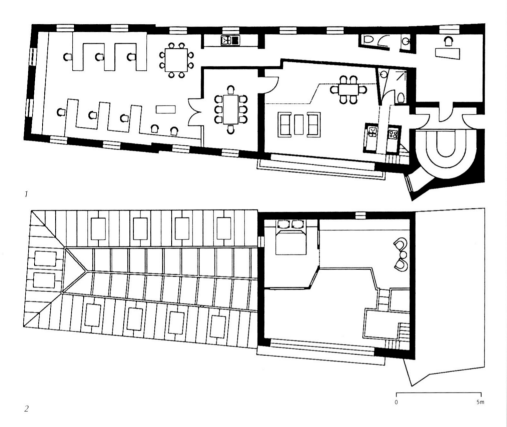

1

2

Perched above a narrow street in the historic core of Vienna is a glass-walled attic, which began life in 1910 as a photographer's studio. The owner of the three-story house sold photographers' supplies on the ground floor, and built the studio for himself and his clients at a time when long exposures required abundant natural light. Miraculously, the glass and its delicate metal frame survived the bombs of 1944 that destroyed a neighboring building and damaged St Stephan's cathedral, a few minutes' walk away. Regina now lives in the 700-square foot studio, next door to her drafting office. The building covers a total of 975 square feet (105 square meters).

To reduce heat loss, the roof was enclosed and insulated, leaving the original steel trusses in the vault. A porthole was inserted in the wall and a square window frames a view of the Peterskirche tower. A free-standing blue cube encloses the kitchen and conceals red stairs leading up to the yellow sleeping gallery; more red stairs lead up to the narrow balcony. The vibrantly colored forms seem to float in the airy void, and the void above the street becomes a second, outdoor room. Returning home on a dark winter's day is like stepping into a hothouse full of exotic blooms.

1 Plan, loft, main floor
2 Plan, loft, upper floor
Opposite:
    Exterior view

4

5

6

4   Living room and kitchen
5   Looking towards bedroom and window overlooking the church tower
6   Close-up of kitchen and red stairs

HOUSE, NIEDERTHAI

Niederthai, Austria
Design/Completion 1994/1996

1

2

3

An hour's drive from Innsbruck, at the heart of Austria's Tirol region, a road winds steeply up to an alpine meadow that's encircled by the village of Niederthai. It's a picture-perfect composition of trees and soaring peaks, grazing cows and wooden chalets. Regina was born here, and returned to build a vacation house for herself and her friends. "The meadow and the mountains were the important things", she says. "It's such a strong, quiet environment, and the spirituality of the places refreshes me every time I go back."

Leon collaborated on the design as Regina did on his house in Schoenfels, and while each home is a response to its setting, personal taste also plays a role. This 836-square foot (90-square meter) house develops ideas first explored in the Villa Petite. It leaps out at you from its site on a knoll at the edge of a forest. Its newly built neighbors rework tradition in a conventional way; the architects have created a taut, wood-framed lodge with a bowed metal roof, white walls, and expansive windows—including a red bay facing out across the meadow. Leading up to the living room terrace is a double flight of yellow stairs that symbolize the earth that was excavated during construction. The house can also be entered from the garage on the far side, and Regina's Citroen *deux chevaux* is an ideal match for its cheerful informality.

The interior comprises a succession of vertiginous stairs linking the main living space to galleries, a suspended yellow bedroom, and the red bay at the top. Unshaded windows on every side frame postcard views, and the open wood vault complements the colored geometry. The stairs invite you to climb and make discoveries, as though you were scrambling up a rock face and finding ledges on which to rest or camp.

Continued...

1   Steps leading up to entrance level
2   Niederthai in its setting of meadow and mountains
3   Regina's Citroen deux chevaux *emerging from garage*
Opposite:
    Exterior front view

Objects are stacked on a stepped balustrade and, because inspiration can strike at any hour, there is a tiny drafting table near the top of the house. "It's meant to be a fun experience", says Regina, "when we spend a weekend here, we find ourselves sitting and talking to each other from different levels, inhabiting the entire space and ignoring conventional room divisions."

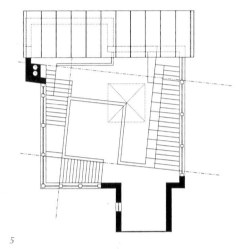

5

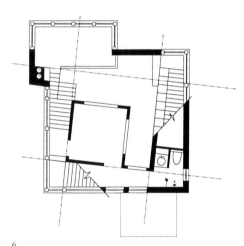

6

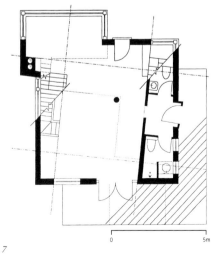

0   5m

7

8

9

Previous page:
Interior of red cube looking out to mountain
5   *Plan, loft*
6   *Plan, upper level*
7   *Plan, ground level*
8   *Looking up the red stairs*
9   *Natural wood ceiling and studio on top of yellow cube*
10 *White steps, yellow cube and models*

10

RÖCKENWAGNER HOUSE

Venice, California, USA
Design/Completion 1996/1997

1

In contrast to the ground-up houses and historically minded remodels Regina and Leon have done in Europe, their recent work in Los Angeles has juggled and expanded on found structures. Bold colors and ingenious new divisions transform a pair of condominium blocks in Santa Monica. A mile south, in the neighboring beach community of Venice, they remodelled a modest wood-framed bungalow for German-born chef Hans Röckenwagner, his fiance, Patti Shin, and his three children.

Hans loves light and space and the existing house had neither. Working within a tight budget and zoning restrictions, the architects gutted the interior, leaving the plain facade and side walls untouched. The original brick hearth, whimsically ornamented with surviving fragments of plaster and floral wallpaper, was left as a free-standing sculpture in the open space that extends back to the garden. New children's rooms flank the entry. Beyond the open kitchen and central dining area the ceiling shoots up, and light floods into a new living room and master suite through picture windows, clerestory openings and skylights. French windows swing open onto a glass-canopied wooden deck, and the back yard is treated as an outdoor room for play and entertaining.

The architects were able to add their trademark red bay to one side of the living room, but the clients picked an intense orange for its lining and painted the curved wall that divides the master suite from the living room a soft yellow that reminds both Hans and Regina of home. These soft tones are set off by white walls and natural wood. As project manager, Tryggvi Thorsteinsson worked closely with Hans to complete construction of the 1,672-square foot (180-square meter) building in four months, leaving the client to complete much of the cabinetry and introduce a personal selection of art works and painted furniture.

0   5   10ft

2

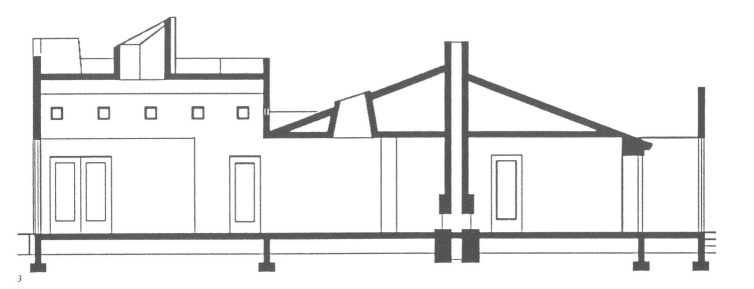

3

4

1   *Rear garden facade*
2   *Floor plan*
3   *Section*
4   *Living area and bedroom*
Following page:
   Living area

6

6   *Looking towards dining room*

TRAH HOUSE

Ippendorf, Bonn, Germany
Design/Completion 1994/1997

1

2

1   Model
2   Garden elevation by night
Opposite:
    Detail of cube and balconies

As Regina and Leon dashed off the Röckenwagner
remodel, they were refining the design and
supervising construction of a 2,982-square foot
(321-square meter) ground-up family house.
A professional couple, Karl and Dagmar Trah,
had bought a hillside plot in an upscale suburban
neighborhood, and requested an expansive house
for themselves and their three small children,

plus home offices where they could work
undisturbed. For the architects, it was a challenge
to fit enough space onto the 40-foot-square
footprint while conforming to design guidelines
that limited the height of the street facade to one
story and regulated the slope of the roof. Several
study models were made before they solved the

Continued...

4

5

4　Top floor with ceiling beams
5　Looking from living room towards family room
6　Stair hall

problem by tucking the children's rooms into the hillside below the living areas, and putting the master suite and two offices above, while concealing this additional story behind a dramatically curved metal roof. The owners have dubbed this their *Schillerlocke*, for the kiss curl of the 18th-century German writer Friedrich von Schiller.

The open-plan main floor serves as common ground and as a buffer between the parents' domain at the top of the house and that of the children, who can walk out of their rooms into the garden. A skylit atrium at the center of the house links the three levels, allowing the parents to look down into the house but be protected from noise by a glass floor in the atrium. A two-

story, south-facing yellow bay floods the living area with light, and frames the landscape, with a distant view of the spires of Cologne Cathedral. The glazing bars on the bay form a Mondrian-like grid. A red kitchen bay adds another splash of color to the white stucco walls. The upstairs rooms are treated as independent volumes that float in the void beneath the steeply vaulted roof, which can be enjoyed throughout the house, and this curve complements the rectilinear volume of the atrium. So well-received was this house that it inspired a similar commission for a plot nearby, and this second house is nearing completion.

Note: these photographs were taken before the house received its colors.

6

7

8

9

7   Living room with glass floor at center
8   Detail, glass floor
9   Living room looking up and out

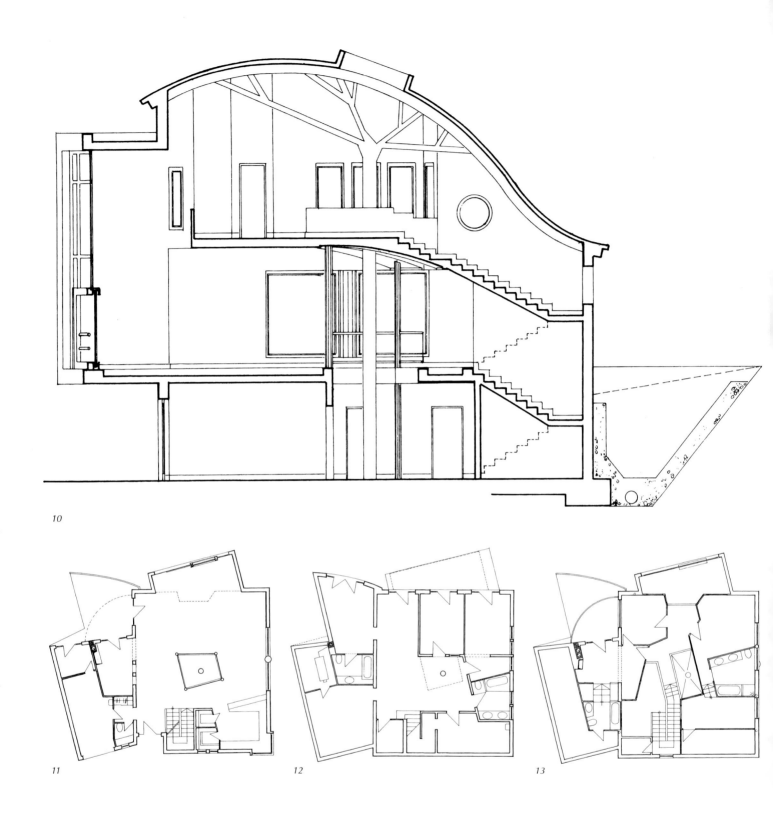

10

11

12

13

10 Section
11 Ground level plan
12 Garden level plan
13 Upper level plan
Opposite:
    Front of cube

Regina Pizzinini

Regina Pizzinini was born in 1959 in Innsbruck, Austria. After graduating from high school in 1977 she attended the University of Innsbruck, gaining a professional degree in architecture and interior design in 1983. While studying she worked in the Tirol office of architect Professor Josef Lackner, and after gaining her degree enrolled in the post-graduate program in architecture at the School of Architecture and Urban Planning, University of California, Los Angeles. While at UCLA she worked part-time as a teaching assistant with Charles Jencks (1984) and research assistant with Charles Moore (1985), as well as working in the Los Angeles office of architects and planners, Moore Ruble Yudell between 1983 and 1985. She received a Master of Architecture degree in 1985, and for the next two years was Assistant Professor, Architecture and Interior Design, Academy for Applied Arts, Vienna. In 1989 she lectured in Building Design with Landscape Studio, UCLA, where she became and still is a visiting critic. Throughout her years of work and study she has made fields trips to Italy, Egypt, northern Europe, California, Mexico, China, Turkey, Yemen and Ghana. She and Leon Luxemburg have conducted a professional practice in Santa Monica and Luxembourg since 1989, working on urban design projects, residential and commercial developments. Their practice in Vienna was established in 1994.

Leon Luxemburg

Leon Glodt was born in Luxembourg in 1955, later taking his birthplace as his professional name in the United States. He gained a degree in civil engineering from the Ecole Supérieure de Technologie du Grand-Duché de Luxembourg in 1977, and a degree in architecture and interior design from the University of Innsbruck, Austria in 1983. He worked in the office of Professor Josef Lackner in Tirol, Austria in 1982, made field trips to Italy, Egypt and the Far East before joining the post-graduate program in urban design at the School of Architecture and Urban Design, University of Houston, Texas, where he was a lecturing assistant before receiving his Master of Urban Design degree in 1984. In 1985 he gained a Master of Architecture degree from the School of Architecture and Urban Planning, University of California, Los Angeles, where he had worked as a teaching assistant with Charles Jencks in 1984, and research assistant with Charles Moore in 1985. From 1983 to 1988 he worked in the Los Angeles office of architects and planners, Moore Ruble Yudell.

Luxembourg office

Los Angeles office
In charge: Tryggvi Thorsteinsson

Luxembourg office
In charge: Daniele Bodson

Vienna office
In charge: Christian Pflegerl

Additional members of the team in Los Angeles, Luxembourg and Vienna:
Reini Köck, Bence Szerdahely, Ian McIlvaine, Aiden Bird, Angelo SanDiego, John Webb, Richard Griswold, David Winans, Jean-Paul Heinen, Myriam Kail, Pit Hoffmann, Vawo Zloic, Linda Retter, Isabelle Quoilin, Alain Werner, Mariana Stoitschkova, Djordje Milosevic, Hannes Bürger, Zaid Abdullatif, Boris Enev, Ivan Toschev, Dimiter Toschev, Atenas Manassiev, Gerhard Höllmüller, Grabner Johanna.

Vienna office

BUILT PROJECTS

(Chronological listing by completion dates)
* Denotes projects featured in this book

2nd Street Apartments, Santa Monica

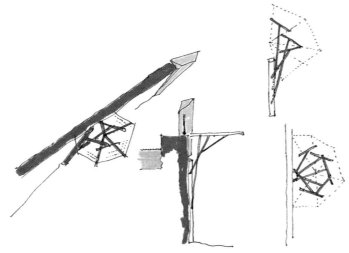

Pool and patio detail, Michel and Jehee Welter, Hollywood

1997

Pool and Patio, Michel and Jehee Welter, Hollywood, California, USA

* Röckenwagner House, Venice, California, USA

* Pizzinini Studio/Apartment, Vienna, Austria

* House, Schoenfels, Luxembourg

1996

* Trah House, Ippendorf, Bonn, Germany

Renovation of Shopping and Entertainment Center, Kaiserpassagen, Bonn, Germany

California Street Apartments, Santa Monica, California, USA

* Kirch Apartments, Mamer, Luxembourg

* Kieffer Photo Studio, City of Luxembourg, Luxembourg

* House, Niederthai, Austria

* Mersch House, City of Luxembourg, Luxembourg

Feidert House, Luxembourg

1995

2nd Street Apartments, Santa Monica, California, USA

1994

* Eich Apartments, City of Luxembourg, Luxembourg

1993

"Healing Waters", Store and Spiritual Center, Beverly Hills, California, USA

* Villa Petite, Bridel, Luxembourg

Corporate Offices for Reinecker Fletcher, Santa Monica, California, USA

First Church of Christ Scientist, World Trade Center, Long Beach, California, USA

Studios for Three Artists, Niederanven, Luxembourg

1992

Spolin and Silverman Law Offices, Santa Monica, California, USA

Addition to Jencks House, Rustic Canyon, Los Angeles, California, USA

House, Malibu Colony, California, USA

* Corman Guest House, Santa Monica, California, USA

1990

First City Texas Bank, Santa Monica, California, USA

Luhring Augustine Hetzler Art Gallery, Santa Monica, California, USA

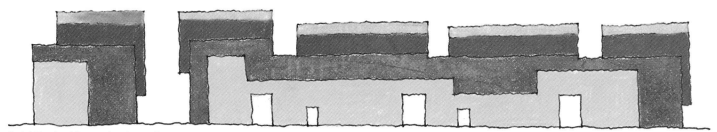

Social Housing, Vienna, elevation study

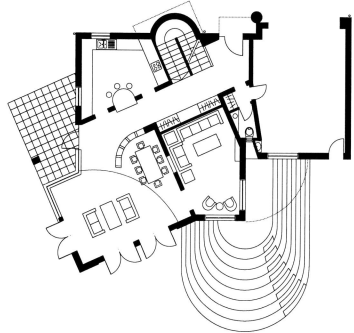

Petin House, Bonn

Fonck Kappweiler House, Luxembourg

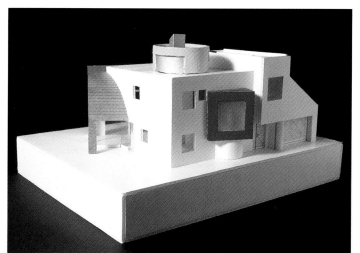

Petin House, Bonn

California Health and Rejuvenation Centers, Los Angeles, California, USA

Edison de Mecco House, Venice, California, USA

Fonck Kappweiler House, Luxembourg

Glen Tobias House, Beverly Hills, California, USA

Hecker House, Luxembourg

Jon Delman House, Pasadena, California, USA

Kremer House, Luxembourg

Marienthal Monastery, Ecological Center, Luxembourg

Petin House, Bonn, Germany

Residential and Student Housing, Vienna, Austria

Sauermillen Vacation Home for the Physically Disabled, Luxembourg

Social Housing, 500 units for the City of Vienna, Austria

Social Housing, Cents, Luxembourg

Urban Design, Martinsplatz, Bonn, Germany

Urban Redevelopment Project, Luxembourg

Wagner-Ley House, Echternach, Luxembourg

Western Museum of Flight, Hawthorne, California, USA

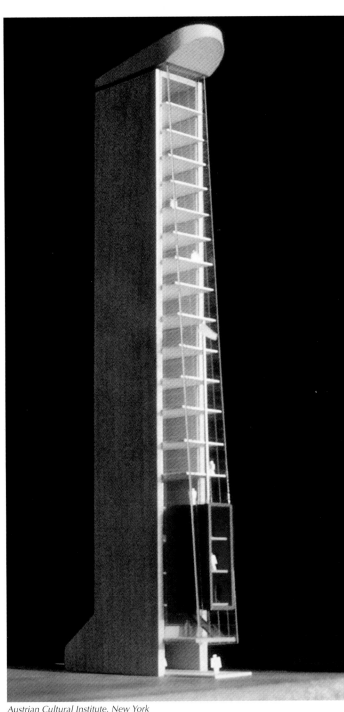

Austrian Cultural Institute, New York

1997

Salle Philharmonique de Luxembourg, Luxembourg

Officers Academy, Enns, Austria

Elementary School and Kindergarten in der Wiesen, Vienna, Austria

1996

Social Housing, Neue Heimat, Innsbruck, Austria

Children's Hospital, Parent–Child Center, Klagenfurt, Austria

1995

Roger Corman Film Studio, Galway, Ireland

1994

Urban Design and Development: Venice Boardwalk, California, USA

1993

Napier House, Mammoth, USA

1992

Boxenbaum House, Mammoth, USA

Austrian Cultural Institute, New York, USA

1991

Olympic Ski Jump Arena, Innsbruck, Austria
    in association with Ove Arup, Los Angeles, USA

1990

"Bettembourg", Master Plan, City Center,
    in association with MRY, Luxembourg

1987

Urban Design, Market Hall and Recreational Facilities, Dudelange,
Luxembourg

Museum Complex in Historical Quarter,
    in association with W. Holzbauer, Vienna, Austria

City Hall and Fire Station, Luxembourg

1986

"Sauerwiss", Master Planning and Social Housing,
    in association with Charles Moore, Luxembourg

Fire Station, Salzburg, Austria

1985

Community Center and Theatre, Tirol, Austria

High School, Graz, Austria

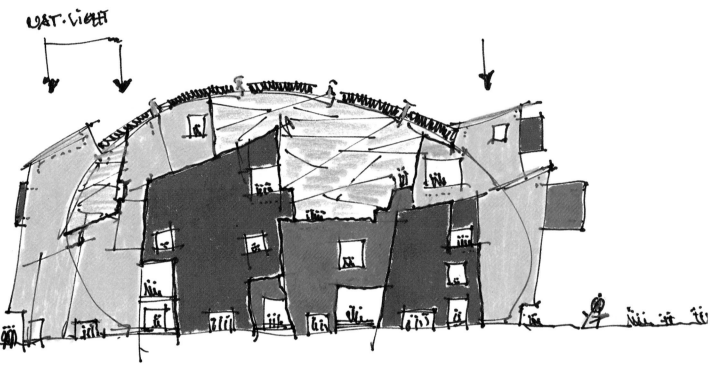

Salle Philharmonique de Luxembourg, Luxembourg

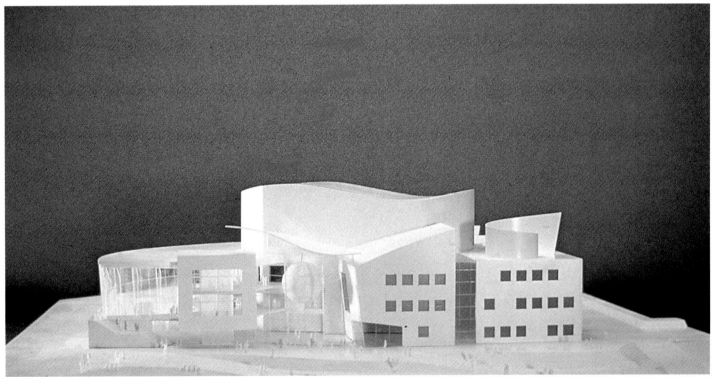

Salle Philharmonique de Luxembourg, Luxembourg

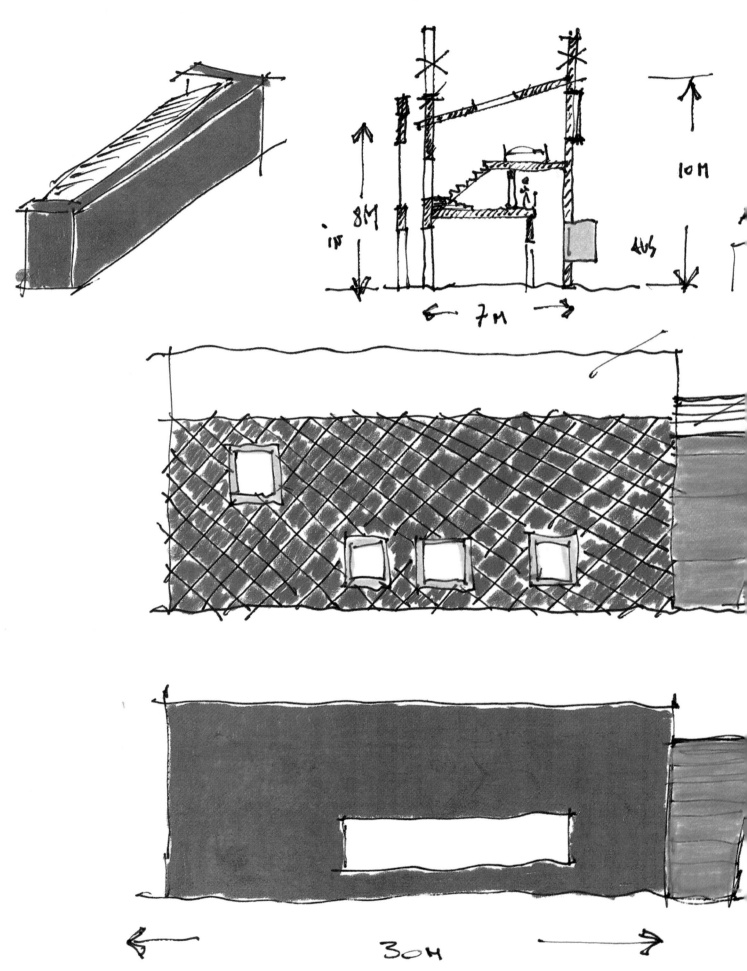

8M

10 M

7M

30M

Roger Corman Film Studio, Galway, elevations

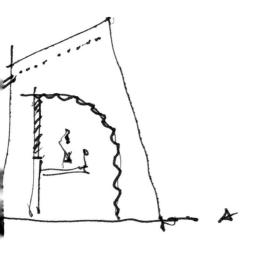

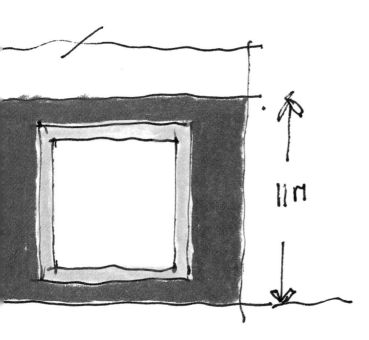

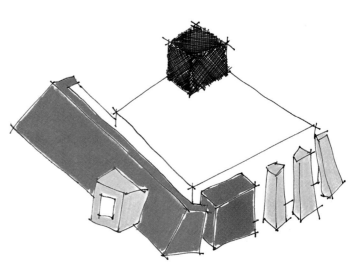

Roger Corman Film Studio, Galway, axonometric

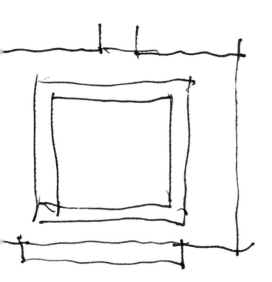

Photography Credits:

Gert von Bassewitz: front cover; 16 (1); 17 (3); 18 (6); 19 (7); 50 (1–3); 51 (4); 52 (5); 54 (8); 55 (10); 70 (1)

Jörg Hemple Photodesign: 62 (2); 63 (3); 64 (4,5); 65 (6); 66 (7); 67 (8,9); 69 (14)

Hill, Douglas: back flap (top)

Jean-Paul Kieffer: 22 (4); 23 (10); 24 (2); 25 (3); 27 (9); 34 (1,2); 35 (3); 38 (7,8)

Yvan Klein: 20 (2); 21 (3); 26 (7,8); 28 (2); 29 (3); 30 (5,6); 32 (10–12); 33 (13); 40 (1,2); 41 (3); 42 (6); 44 (7–9); 62 (1); 71 (1)

Erhard Pfeiffer: rear cover; 57 (4); 58 (5); 60 (6)

Jeremy Samuelson: 56 (1)

Rupert Steiner: 46 (3); 48 (4); 49 (5,6); 71 (2)

Undine Prohl: 72 (1)

Dominique Vorillon: 12 (1); 13 (3); 14 (4,5); 15 (6)

Michael Webb: 9 (1); 10 (1,2); 11 (2); 54 (9)

BIBLIOGRAPHY

"Abstraction—Regina Pizzinini & Leon Luxemburg", *Paradise Transformed: The private garden for the twenty-first century,* The Monacelli Press, 1996 New York

"Architektur: Villa Kunterbunt jetzt mit Grundriss", *Häuser,* March 1994, Germany

"Color it Corman", *Elle Decor,* November 1991, New York

Cover, *Casa Vogue,* N.251, April 1994, Italy

"Drawings by Architects", *ZYZZYVA,* cultural magazine, 1991, San Francisco

"Ein Haus bekennt Farbe", *Schöner Wohnen,* June 1993, Germany

"Einmal anders wohnen", *TT,* March 1988, Austria

"Impulse", *Architektur in Tirol,* Austria, 1982

"Los Angeles", *Abitare,* May 1994, AIA Los Angeles Centennial Celebration Edition, 1994 AIA Convention Issue

"Manifest 2000", *Cafe Creme,* 1989, Luxembourg

"Masterplan Urban Design", *Baumeister,* 1991, Germany

"Mehr als Farben", *Revue,* March 1997, Luxembourg

"Mehr Farbe: frisch und frech", *Immobilien,* 1994, Munich, Germany

"Mut zum Mini", *Häuser,* June 1996, Germany

"Pizzini–Luxemburg", article and cover on Corman Guest House, *Interior Architecture,* No. 37, 1993, Australia

"Positive Aura", *Architektur,* Österreichisches Fachmagazin, September 1996, Vienna

"Reflections on Urbanism", *European periodical,* 1993, Luxembourg

"Schutzhuette aus einer anderen Welt", *Der Alpinist,* September 1983, Germany

"Short-Order Remodel", *Los Angeles Times Magazine,* October 1997

"Uberhaupt nicht Kleinkariert", *Architektur,* December 1996, Vienna

"Urban Projects: Luxembourg Cultural City 1995", *Revue Technique,* 1993, Luxembourg

"Variationen in Rot-Blau-Gelb", *Telecran 42,* October 1997, Luxembourg

"Villa Petite", *Award Winning Architecture,* International Yearbook, 1997, Germany

INDEX
Bold page numbers refer to featured projects